PETER SCULTHORPE

Mountains

for solo piano

 FABER ***ff*** MUSIC

© 1982 by Faber Music Ltd
First published in 1982 by Faber Music Ltd
3 Queen Square London WC1N 3AU
Music drawn by Sheila Stanton
Cover design by Shirley Tucker
Printed in England by Caligraving Ltd
All rights reserved

ISBN 0-571-50661-5

The publication of this score has been assisted
by a grant from the Music Board of the Australia Council

To buy Faber Music publications or to find out about the full range of titles available
please contact your local music retailer or Faber Music sales enquiries:

Faber Music Limited, Burnt Mill, Elizabeth Way, Harlow, CM20 2HX England
Tel: +44 (0)1279 82 89 82   Fax: +44 (0)1279 82 89 83
sales@fabermusic.com   www.fabermusic.com

Mountains was commissioned by the Sydney International Piano Competition, 1981,
with assistance from the Music Board of the Australia Council.
It was first performed by Gabriella Pusner in Verbrugghen Hall,
Sydney Conservatorium of Music, on 4 July 1981.

The work is a response to the mountainous terrain of Tasmania,
often known as 'Isle of Mountains', where the composer was born.

Duration: approx. 5 minutes

To Rex Hobcroft

Mountains

PETER SCULTHORPE

molto cresc.

Sydney, January 1981